# Railways & Recollections

Gentlemen

Waiting room
Ladies

Departures

Motorail

# Contents

## Series Introduction

Welcome to a brand new and innovative series!

Railway publishing has been around almost as long as the railways themselves and there have been countless books with a historical theme, telling the story of a particular line, say, and occasionally linking the subject to its social context, but never before has there been, in such an accessible way, a juxtapositioning of photographic illustration of a railway subject with the events, happenings and highlights of a wider sphere and calendar. This series will, initially, take a particular year and place the views displayed alongside a carefully selected pot-pourri of what happened in that twelve-month period. The vast majority of the images in the first few books are from the Ray Ruffell collection, held by the publisher, but material from other sources will be interspersed where felt necessary

to maintain appropriate variety. Ray was a railwayman and photographer of equal merit and the main criterion for inclusion in these books is for the images to be both interesting and aesthetically pleasing within a chosen theme.

The books are aimed at a more general market than mere railway aficionados or enthusiasts and the authors hope and trust that they will be sure in their aim and that you, the reader, will find much to enjoy, appreciate, enthuse about and even smile about! And it is hoped that some of your own memories are stirred along the way and that you may wish to share these with friends!

© John Stretton and Peter Townsend 2006
Photos: © The NOSTALGIA Collection archive unless otherwise credited.

First published in 2006
ISBN 1 85794 276 0　 ISBN 978 1 85794 276 7
Silver Link Publishing Ltd
The Trundle
Ringstead Road
Great Addington
Kettering
Northants NN14 4BW

Tel/Fax: 01536 330588
email: sales@nostalgiacollection.com
Website: www.nostalgiacollection.com
British Library Cataloguing in Publication Data
A catalogue record for this book is available from the British Library.
Printed and bound in Great Britain.

*Above* **ALDERSHOT** Once a common scene but so much has since disappeared over the past 30 years or so, including semaphore signals, the water tower, signalbox and even the 'slam-door' stock retreating from this view

*Frontispiece* Sights such as this are no longer possible on our railways but – and it may come as a surprise to many – a Motorail service still ran in the 21st century, operated by First Great Western between Penzance and Paddington. However, as with other demands for care and comfort in our modern society, the vehicles are now transported under cover, in specially converted coaching stock, while the drivers sit or sleep in the Night Riviera Sleeper services. In our year, facilities were a little more basic, as can be judged from this view. Thought to be Reading (General) station, the consist includes a Morris 1800, a Vauxhall Viva Estate, a Mercedes with German (D) country sticker a Ford Consul/Granada, and at least one Austin 1100.

# Introduction
## Railways & Recollections 1973

On the world stage, it was a case of more 'downs' than 'ups' in 1973. The US and North Vietnam signed a peace treaty; Britain joined the European Economic Community; and the US World Trade Centre opened; but, to counter these positives, Israel defeated the Arabs in the Yom Kippur War; General Pinochet overthrew the Allende government in Chile; and the Persian Gulf States doubled the price of oil! This latter was to have massive ramifications worldwide, not least in the UK, where petrol ration coupons were introduced in November and the three-day-week was announced in December, to curb the use of power. Elsewhere, the price of gold reached an all-time closing price on 5 June – at $126 per ounce on the London market; and the UK Government introduced VAT for the first time with the March budget, initially at 10%.

Personalities born this year were illusionist David Blaine, White House intern Monica Lewinsky, and tennis stars Greg Rusedski and Monica Seles. Elsewhere in entertainment, the FA Cup proved to be a day remembered by many for years to come outside of the two teams' supporters, when Sunderland, from the 2nd Division beat 1st Division opponents Leeds United 1-0!

In music, the year opened with Sweet's Blockbuster, at No.1 for five weeks, followed by Slade's Cum On Feel The Noize. This latter group then ended the year at the top with the seasonal (and ever popular) Merry Christmas Everybody. Along the way, there were six other entries that stayed at No.1 for four weeks – Tie A Yellow Ribbon Round The Old Oak Tree (Dawn), See My Baby Jive (Wizard), I'm The Leader Of The Gang (Gary Glitter), Young Love (Donny Osmond), Eye Level (Simon Park Orchestra) and I Love You Love Me Love (Gary Glitter). Single sales were beginning to slip, however, with albums sales and charts assuming greater importance. 'Various Artists' compilations featured strongly during the year, but long-term chart topping was achieved by Elton John (Don't Shoot I'm Only The Piano Player – 6 weeks) and David Bowie (Pin Ups – 5 weeks).

One might have thought that the Beeching cuts would have so decimated our railway system that there was precious little left to dispense with, but 65 closures were still made during the year! A majority were freight and/or industrial lines and connections – such as Harpur Hill-Hindlow and Hillhead Quarry (near Buxton), Whitwood-Aire & Calder Chemical Works, Wadebridge-Wadebridge Quay,

*(Continued on page 4)*

*Background* **EASTLEIGH** Extensive marshalling yards are now, largely, a thing of the past. Shunting, shuffling and re-arranging thousands of wagons annually at such locations was a logistical nightmare for the authorities and hard work for the men on the ground. This is Eastleigh on 6 February, when the practice was still widespread. An unidentified Class 47 diesel passes the station.

High Dyke-Sproxton and Port Meadow New Spur Jct-Rewley Road Exchange Sidings in Oxford – but passenger services also suffered between Alton and Winchester, Botley and Farnham and Daly and Kilmarnock. TOPS was introduced, which over a couple of years totally transformed the numbering of BR's locomotives away from the 1957 blocks of D1-D9999 and E1-E9999. Where the new numbers did not follow the previous chronological orders, it initially brought much confusion to the enthusiast and rail worker alike. Depots were also reclassified, with letters instead of the old number series. E.g. Toton (once 18A, but 16A between 9/63 and 5/73) became TO, but not all easily fitted the new way and some, like Thornaby, took a slightly obscure persona (ex-51L from 6/58-5/73 becoming TE).

*John Stretton*
*Oxfordshire*

*Peter Townsend*
*Northamptonshire*

*April 2006*

# 1973
# Diesel shunters at work

Left **EASTLEIGH** Another, more close-up view of Eastleigh yard on 6 February. Some yards had dedicated, specially designed shunters to handle the work but, elsewhere, 'bog standard' locos were used. Here we have examples of both. To the left, 'ordinary' shunter 3010 - later classified 08 - rests alongside slightly less powerful 2995, to become Class 07. Both have lost their previous 'D' number appendages and would be renumbered within a year under BR's new TOPS (Total Operations Processing System) renumbering scheme, introduced this year.

Above **WATERLOO** The type that became BR Class 08 under TOPS had been introduced way back in 1952 but was still giving invaluable service 20 years later. Surrounded by electric units, 1961-vintage No. 4111 coasts towards Waterloo station with the 09.36 'milk' from Clapham Junction on 29 June.

*Left* **WATERLOO** Another '08' outside Waterloo on 29 June. With the 13.20 to Portsmouth Harbour departing behind it, No. 4005 stands waiting the next call to duty.

New from Derby Works in December 1960, the ex-D4005 was to become 08837 eight months after this view under the TOPS renumbering. Looking remarkably clean in this portrait, it was withdrawn from official records in November 2005 and scrapped a month later.

*Right* **WATERLOO** No.4111, seen on p.5 on 29 June, is here again at work at Waterloo on the following day. It is now in company with fellow classmate 4114 and has acquired a coach as well as the milk tanker as the quartet stand in Platform 15. Beyond, EMU 4SUB No. 4112 is trapped at the buffer stops.

Sadly, like so much other freight business throughout our railway system, this milk traffic has long been lost to road transport. Note the parcels trolleys on both platforms – sadly, another sight that has largely disappeared – and the wonderfully intricate steel tracery of the Victorian trainshed at this terminus.

# 1973
## Happenings (1)

- UK, Denmark and Ireland join EEC (January)

- George Foreman wins against Joe Frazier ending his undefeated world heavyweight boxing champion record (January)

- Richard Nixon re-elected US President (January)

- Vietnam ceasefire agreed (January)

- Vietnam War ends with the signing of peace pacts (27 January)

- Archbishop Makarios re-elected as Cypriot President (February)

- The London Stock Exchange allows women traders (March)

- Vote in Northern Ireland to stay in the United Kingdom (March)

- HM Queen Elizabeth II opens the new London Bridge (March)

- British Governor of Bermuda and Assistant Governor assassinated (March)

- Richard Nixon resigns US Presidency (April)

*Left* **WATERLOO** Our final look at Waterloo's shunters shows the front end of No.4005 at the buffer stops on 28 June. Fairly recently painted from this view, the yellow and black warning stripes surround the radiator grille and, on the far side, the vacuum pipes stand ready to connect to appropriate stock. An excellent view for those railway modellers wishing to add super detail to their model!

*Opposite inset* **LITTLE SANDHURST** Progressively over the previous two decades, multiple units – both diesel and, where possible, electric – replaced steam hauled stock, mostly on branch line workings but even on longer distance turns.

On 8 July, WR Class 117 DMU set L (for London) 412 passes the delightful tree-lined avenue near Little Sandhurst with the 10.23 Reading-Blackwater & Camberley stopping service.

*Opposite main* Just over three months earlier, the avenue is not quite so appealing, with grass and tree leaf not yet recovered from the effects of winter. On 25 March, a Metro-Cammell three-car DMU set 410 is an example of some longer journeys undertaken – with less space and comfort for the traveller! – as it works a Wolverhampton-East Croydon Special!

Note the difference between the styles of headcode (destination indicators) between the two units on this page

# 1973
# Multiple Units
# on manoeuvres

*Main picture* **LITTLE SANDHURST** As well as the DMUs and EMUs already seen, there were also DEMUs – Diesel-Electric Multiple Units! – the difference being the unit traction was electrically driven as opposed to mechanically on the DMUs (which technically should be known as D<u>M</u>MUs!). Set No.1206 – known as a 'Tadpole' Unit, due to the disparity of body width between the ex 2EPB EMU Driving Trailer (nearest the camera here) and the slimmer Hastings gauge DEMU pair behind – with an appropriate SR headcode for the route, is another return shuttle to Reading, being the 11.50 from Blackwater & Camberley on 8 July. The history of the 'Tadpole' nickname is too long and complicated for space available in this volume!

*Inset* **LITTLE SANDHURST** Class 117 DMU set L412, seen on p.9, is again seen passing Little Sandhurst on 8 July, forming the 12.10 return Blackwater & Camberley-Reading service. On this day the service from Reading was truncated at Blackwater, due to engineering works on the track towards Farnborough. The '2A05' code is an indicator to signallers and station staff of the specific service and here means '2' – ordinary or branch passenger train, 'A' – WR London Area working, '05' a sequential number for trains that day.

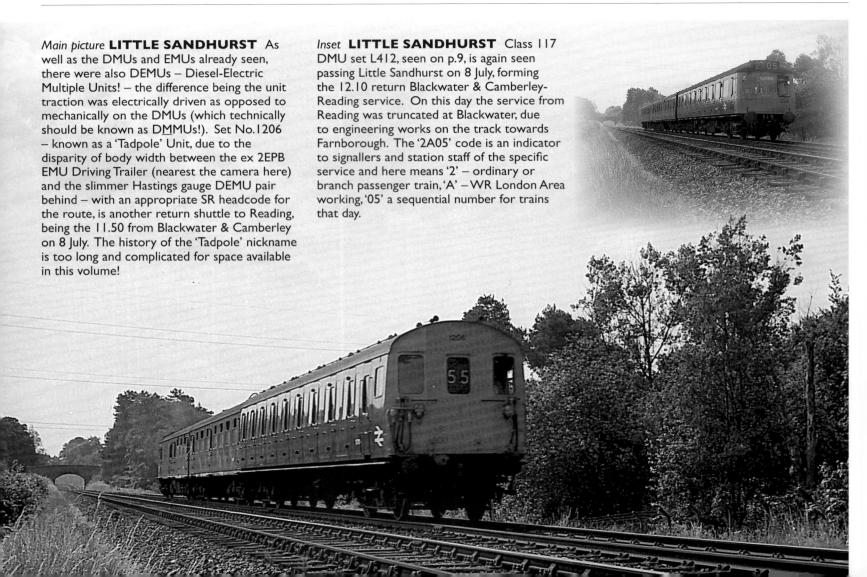

# 1973
## Happenings (2)

- World Trade Center officially opens
  in New York                              (April)

- One day national strike in Britain on May Day

- First visit to Israel by German Chancellor
  (Willy Brandt)                           (May)

- Three Royal Navy Frigates deployed
  to protect fishing fleet in "Cod War"    (May)

- Greek government vote to replace
  Monarchy with Republic                   (June)

- Russian Tupolev 144 crashes at Paris
  airshow killing 14 people                (June)

- George Papoudopolos becomes
  first President of Greece                 (August)

**PORTSMOUTH HARBOUR** Yet another DMU styling is represented by WR B (for Bristol) 578, seen at Portsmouth Harbour on 15 July. Outward appearances would seem to indicate that the unit had recently been through the carriage washer and perhaps this is connected with the fact that it is here waiting to provide accommodation as a Special Charter to Salisbury. Perhaps some of the participants will avail themselves of the 'Trophy Bitter' advertised at the far end of Platform 1!?!

**WINDERMERE** As previously mentioned, multiple units were introduced in an attempt to cut costs, especially on branch lines. They were successful in saving many such lines but not necessarily the infrastructure. Windermere station, the terminus of the erstwhile Kendal & Windermere Railway branch from Oxenholme, was once graced with two main platforms (under cover – see also p.42) and at least four other platform faces. As can be seen in this view of a DMU departing for the other end of the line, time has not been kind! By 2006, all that remains is the platform being used here by the unit, with Booth's supermarket occupying the old station building (to the rear of the photographer).

*Above* **WATERLOO** What looks to be a rare beast lurking inside Waterloo station in September is, in truth, one of a pair of prototype units – introduced in 1971 – that broke the mould of previous thought. Unique at the time, the PEP units included innovations that have since become standard, such as sliding doors, sloping body profile, open plan inside and front end design with just a central buffer arrangement that included electronics. Here in unpainted aluminium, all cars were powered giving high acceleration and they were tested on the routes to Shepperton, Hampton Court and Chessington.

*Left* **WATERLOO** The poor old 4SUB No. 4112 seen on p.7, trapped by the buffer stops at Waterloo, is again seen here a few minutes later on 30 June. With Nationalisation in 1948, BR(SR) inherited the largest live rail network in the UK.

The Southern Railway had instituted a programme of new-build and this was continued with a fleet of all steel, high-density slam door units designed by Oliver Bullied that became the most numerous of any on the SR. 4112 was the first of the batch constructed in 1946 and by our year was being overtaken by more modern design ideas (see p.13).

*Right* **GLASGOW (CENTRAL)** More attractive steel tracery but at the other end of the country. Local set 133 has doors open ready for intending passengers for the '2K76' service to Kilmacolm, now a terminus but once on a through route to Greenock.

Passenger services beyond Kilmacolm ceased from 2 February 1959 and even the remaining section was closed ten years after this view. The 'sister' set 144 to the right was to be a working to Ardrossan. Judging by the condition of the platform, left, the station canopy was not wholly waterproof!

# 1973
# Arrivals & Departures

**Births**

| Caroline Corr | musician | | 17 March |
| David Blaine | magician | | 4 April |
| Sachin Tendulkar | Indian cricketer | | 24 April |
| Leigh Francis | comedian | | 30 May |
| Monica Lewinsky | White House intern | | 23 July |
| Darren Campbell | athlete | | 12 September |
| Robert Pires | footballer | | 29 October |
| Ryan Giggs | footballer | | 29 November |
| Paula Radcliffe | athlete | | 7 April |

**Deaths**

| Lyndon Johnson | US President | (b. 1908) | 22 January |
| Edward G. Robinson | actor | (b. 1893) | 26 January |
| Noel Coward | composer/playwright | (b. 1899) | 26 March |
| Pablo Picasso | artist | (b. 1881) | 8 April |
| Betty Grable | actress | (b 1916) | 3 July |
| Fulgencio Batista | Cuban dictator | (b. 1901) | 6 August |
| J. R. R. Tolkien | writer | (b. 1892) | 2 September |
| David Ben-Gurion | Israeli Prime Minister | (b. 1886) | 1 December |
| Bobby Darin | singer | (b. 1936) | 20 December |

**LITTLE SANDHURST** Our final look at the units shows yet another type at Little Sandhurst, this time on 10 June but the service still badly affected by the track relaying at Blackwater & Camberley. Swindon 'Inter City' Class 123 unit L709 passes the back gardens, en route from Reading.

*Pages 18-19* **ALDERSHOT** Words are superfluous! Just enjoy the wonderful panoramic view from the signalbox of some of the visual delights that our railway system used to provide! In the case of the water tower this can still be enjoyed, having been reconstructed at Alton on The Mid Hants Railway.

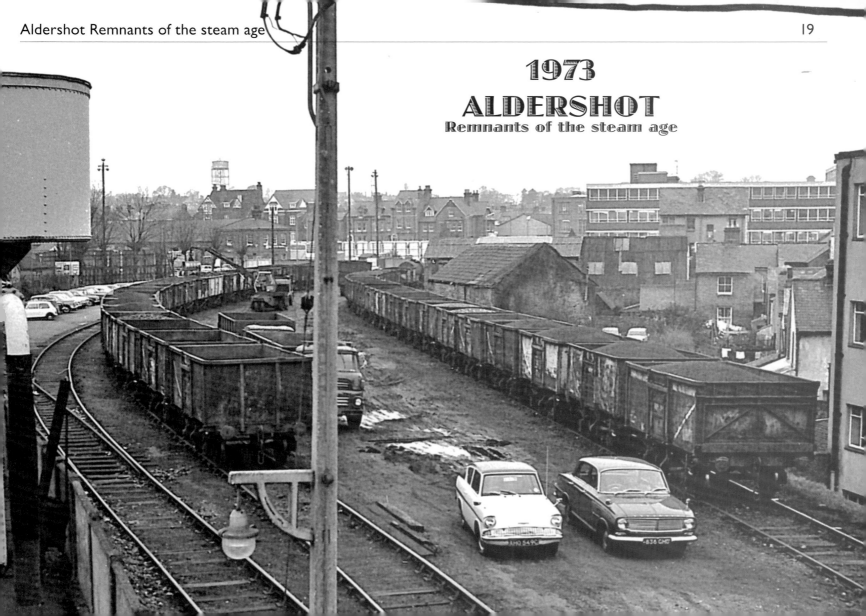

# 1973
# ALDERSHOT
Remnants of the steam age

*Left* **ALDERSHOT** Two more examples of items of infrastructure, once so common, that have now largely vanished from the scene. A slam-door unit waits in Aldershot station for its time to leave, with the way forward sanctioned by the skyward pointing semaphore, atop its lattice post. Note also the water tank, still ready to serve nearly a decade after steam ended on this part of the SR!

*Below* **ALDERSHOT** Over 70 years since its installation, the 24-levered ex-L&SWR signalbox is still open. Note the bricked-up windows in the base housing the Stevens frame, and the annexe by the stairs, for the signalman's convenience!

# 1973
# The Electrics are spreading!

*Previous page* **PRESTON** The headboard on Class 87 electric No. 87002 says it all. The date is 23 July and this is the first day of electric services between Euston and this far north on the West Coast Main Line (WCML). Platform end spotters are obviously interested in this new development, but the 'old order', in the guise of Class 40 No. 323, still solicits some interest from the trio of lads on the far platform face.

*Left and right* **PRESTON** Two more views of the 'new order' on 23 July. No. 87002, in plain corporate blue with full yellow ends, stands in the bay platform, polished and buffers burnished for its admiring public! The enthusiasts are keen to examine the interloper and to see what is inside the cab! Less than a month out of Crewe Works on this date, it remained 'anonymous' until 3 July 1978, when it was named *Royal Sovereign* at Willesden depot. Thirty two years on and fortunes have not been wholly kind to the '87s', with their duties taken over by Richard Branson's Virgin Trains' 'all-singing, all-dancing, all-tilting' 'Pendolinos'. 87002's life, however, was longer than 323 in the other platform. Introduced in May 1961 – to sweep away front-line steam out of Euston – it was itself, in turn, swept from the WCML by the electrics and eked out its life around Edinburgh. The end came at Haymarket depot, in the city, on 7 July 1980, after a life of less than twenty years. Not exactly an investment triumph for BR!

# 1973
## Happenings (3)

- Summerland fire in Douglas IOM over 40 people lose their lives (August)

- Henry Kissinger becomes US Secretary of State (September)

- Len Murray elected as president of TUC (September)

- Yom Kippur War breaks out between Israel, Egypt and Syria (October)

- Sydney Opera House opened by HM The Queen (October)

- LBC and Capital Radio launched (October)

- UK Fuel Crisis deepens state of emergency declared (November)

- Royal Wedding Princess Anne marries Captain Mark Phillips (November)

- Three Day week introduced by Edward Heath's Government (December)

- TOPS (Total Operations Processing System) numbering introduced on British Railways

- Space Vehicle patent filed by British Railways Board granted (March)

*Left* **PRESTON** The electrics are coming – as evidenced by the proliferation of 25kV a.c. wires and supporting stanchions (newly erected judging by the detritus on the ground!) – but DMUs still found lucrative business. Various sets making up eight coaches, begin to slow for the station stop at Preston on 23 July, with a northbound holiday special bound for Blackpool.

*Opposite* **BRIGHTON** Like Blackpool, the destination in the previous picture, seaside towns were helped to grow and develop with the coming of the railway and, in turn, they provided much valuable traffic for the relevant companies. This continued under BR, the length and breadth of the country. This is the view of Brighton (Central) station on 28 March – not a time of massive influx of holidaymakers, but still extremely busy morning and evening with local commuters. The time is mid-morning and all is relaxed compared to just a couple of hours earlier. A porter steers his motorised trolley towards the ranks of parcel trolleys, with, alongside on Platform 7, piles of mailbags await attention. Note yet more intricate steel tracery and supporting fluted pillars.

British Rail Brighton

1973
Down by the sea

*Opposite top, left to right* **BRIGHTON** A vital and, thankfully, ever-present provision on larger stations, was the newspaper kiosk – here supplied by W H Smith & Son. Many are 'walk-in' today, but that is a relatively recent innovation. The four-sided ex-LB&SCR station clock, hopefully showing the same time on all sides! 'The Railway Bell', a nearby hostelry with a slightly more imaginative name and sign than the more common 'The Railway...'.

*Left lower* **BRIGHTON** Out on the seafront, a young enthusiast watches the 1883-vintage Volks Railway, with a 'train' retreating into the distance, on 28 March. Obviously, this early spring day is not as warm as it might be!

*Right* **BRIGHTON** The country end of Brighton station on 28 March. The units are close in number but of different generations. Four-car Class 411 4CEP No. 7109, new in September 1958 and renumbered 1527 in April 1981 waits to honour its '12' headcode by running a semi-fast service to Victoria. Its front end appears cluttered and ugly compared to its younger companion.

Class 421 4CIG No. 7369, also four-car, was similarly later renumbered, to 1269 in May 1987; it has recently arrived from Victoria. What could be the driver of 7109 briefly pauses to chat with someone just a few feet from the cab door.

**BRIGHTON** Three more views of Brighton.
*Left upper* A station of a different kind! Close
to the terminus of the Volks Railway, the
Aquarium Station gives access to swimming and
eating!

*Left lower* The cars of the VR seem empty on
this chilly 28 March day, but the facility has
survived to 2006, to celebrate its 123rd year.

*Below* The imposing twin trainshed canopies
peer defiantly above the spacious station
entrance.

# 1973
# Roaming Devon rails

**DAWLISH** The summer has passed and the holidaymakers have returned home and the beach is empty. The sun is shining brightly on this 2 October day, but there is a wind causing some white caps on the waves, as an unidentified Class 47 heads south away from Dawlish. Earlier in the year, this stretch of coastline, with its famous sea wall, would have had plenty of observers of the passing trains. *John Stretton collection*

# 1973
## FILMS - A SELECTION

| Title | Director |
|-------|----------|
| • The Sting | George Roy Hill |
| • Badlands | Terrence Malick |
| • American graffiti | George Lucas |
| • Papillon | Franklin J Schaffner |
| • Enter the dragon | Robert Clouse |
| • Mean streets | Martin Scorsese |
| • The long goodbye | Robert Altman |
| • The Wicker Man | Robin Hardy |
| • Don't look now | Nicolas Roegl |
| • Sleeper | Woody Allen |
| • Serpico | Sidney Lumet |
| • The Exorcist | William Friedkin |
| • Pat Garrett and Billy The Kid | Sam Peckinpah |

**DAWLISH**  Two days earlier, on 30 September, the weather is still bright and sunny and the sea is calm. The tide is fully in, however, leaving no sand on which to sit and enjoy the views, but as there are few people enjoying a stroll along the sea wall, no-one will be complaining!  On the thin strip of railway land between sea and town, an unidentified 'Western' (BR Class 52) locomotive hauls its ten-coach load south through Dawlish station without stopping. *John Stretton collection*

**DAWLISH** Slightly later in the day, on 30 September, storm clouds appear to be gathering from the south as another unidentified Class 47 passes Dawlish station without stopping, this time heading north, probably on a 'cross-country' working, possibly to Liverpool, rather than making for London. A little short of three years later and these views would largely be extinguished, as the then brand new HST rakes were introduced between Paddington and Plymouth/Penzance. *John Stretton collection*

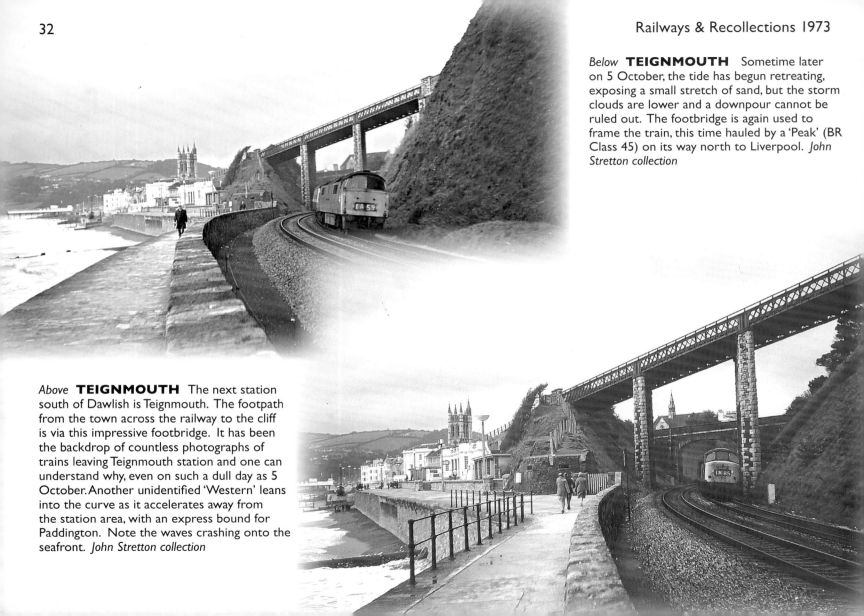

*Below* **TEIGNMOUTH** Sometime later on 5 October, the tide has begun retreating, exposing a small stretch of sand, but the storm clouds are lower and a downpour cannot be ruled out. The footbridge is again used to frame the train, this time hauled by a 'Peak' (BR Class 45) on its way north to Liverpool. *John Stretton collection*

*Above* **TEIGNMOUTH** The next station south of Dawlish is Teignmouth. The footpath from the town across the railway to the cliff is via this impressive footbridge. It has been the backdrop of countless photographs of trains leaving Teignmouth station and one can understand why, even on such a dull day as 5 October. Another unidentified 'Western' leans into the curve as it accelerates away from the station area, with an express bound for Paddington. Note the waves crashing onto the seafront. *John Stretton collection*

# 1973
# Loco hauled freight

**EASTLEIGH** There are still loco-hauled freights on our railway system today, but, undoubtedly, there is not the variety that was once enjoyed. Car transportation still occurs, but, again, there have been shifts of fortune for many of the previous flows. On 6 February, nine-year old 'Brush 4' No. 1553 (later BR Class 47) moves its '4E00' (express freight for the Eastern region) train forward and prepares to leave Eastleigh yard, en route to Ripple Lane in east London. Renumbered 47437 in December under TOPS, it was withdrawn from Crewe Diesel depot on 7 April 1987.

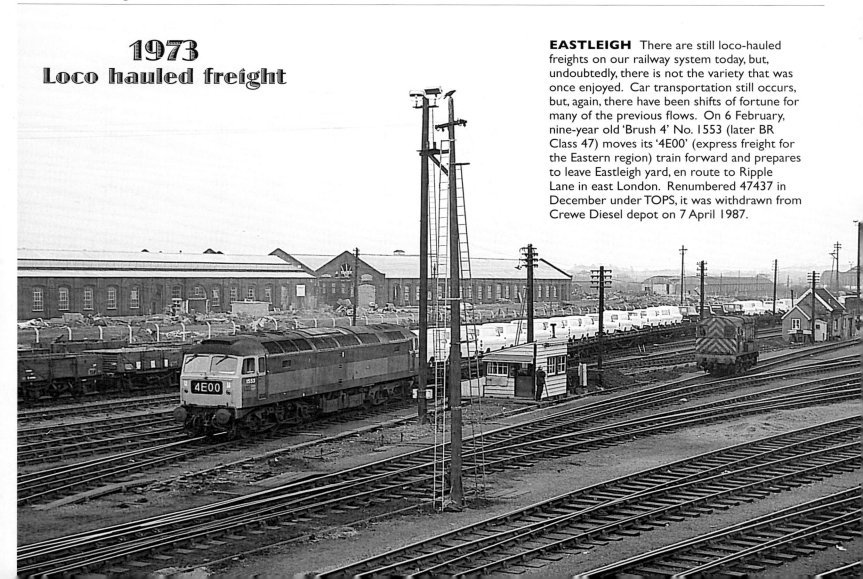

*Below* **WOKING** In addition to coal, a major source of revenue for BR was the transhipment of stone, either for ballast or for road construction. There were centres in Leicestershire and elsewhere, but two of the most important sources were from quarries south of Westbury. On 15 May, Class 47 No. 1729 heads south at Woking with a rake of empty stone hoppers, from Merstham, between Redhill and Coulsdon, to Westbury.

*Opposite* **BARNES** While the top-flight main line diesels did not commonly operate freight trains at this time, the often slightly less powerful, 'mixed traffic' types held sway. One such is seen from the cab of an EMU, between Barnes and Putney on a dull 27 June. Snapped at 1/200th of a second at f5.6, BR Type 2 (later Class 25) No. 5216 is obviously hard at work, hauling a loaded rake of fully fitted coal wagons. Note the live third rail, to the right and slightly raised above the running rails. With his hand at the cab window, one wonders whether the second man is acknowledging or hiding his face!

**GUILDFORD** Always wishing to be different – and thereby following in GWR's footsteps! – BR(WR) opted for diesel hydraulic transmission for their designs, as opposed to diesel electric for the rest of the system. While a good design and largely reliable, they were non-standard and were, therefore, subject to early withdrawal. The Hymeks were stylish, as can be judged in this view of No. 7018 at Guildford on 18 December. Code '4016' – indicating a parcels train bound for the SR – was a daily working between Bradford (Exchange) and Redhill and no doubt is here full of Christmas goodies! New in January 1962, 7018 only survived until March 1975 on BR's books but, happily, thereafter found salvation and a new home in preservation on the West Somerset Railway.

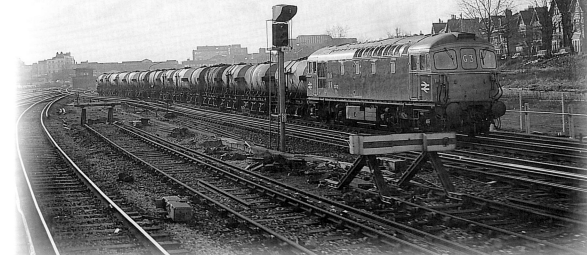

*Below* **WIMBLEDON** Having seen Type 2s from the Western and Eastern Regions, we now see one indigenous to the Southern. What was to become BR Class 33s were introduced in 1960, for second link passenger and routine freight duties and while a fixture on Southern metals throughout their BR existence, they worked the early Cliffe-Uddington (south of Glasgow) cement, Portsmouth-Cardiff and Cardiff-Crewe passenger services and could be seen as far west as Haverfordwest. In attractive photographic winter light on 2 February 1974, hauling the Morden-Clapham milk tanks past Wimbledon, No. 33112 (ex-6529) was one of the first of the class to be renumbered, in December 1973.

*Above* **GUILDFORD** It has always been the case that, on the normal railway – i.e. apart from special workings – one can never be quite sure what will come along next. Thus, in this view of the '4016' parcels train seen on p.36, the motive power is different. Presumably Hymek No. 7018, being a WR engine, would at some point have replaced a locomotive that had brought the consist from Bradford (Exchange), whereas in this view the following day, Type 2 (later Class 31) No. 5686, being an ER loco, has possibly worked right through from original departure.

**THE 'PEAKS'** – thus known from the names of the early machines celebrating some of the highest peaks in the UK – later to be BR Class 44/45, were truly mixed traffic locos, able to handle virtually any traffic given to them. The first Peak numerically D1 *Scafell Pike** was named appropriately after the highest peak in England.

*\* One of your authors (PT) has a certificate for NOT climbing to the top of this peak, the hill not the loco; his wife Frances intends to climb to the top before her 50th birthday in July 2006!*

*Below* **READING** On 21 July, No. 135 skirts around the northern side of Reading (General) station with a mixed rake of vans and low loaders carrying concrete sleepers, the '8Z42' code indicating a through freight not operating as an express service, the '8' and as a special, i.e. not scheduled, working, the 'Z'.

*Right* **KEW BRIDGE** Another Class 8 freight is seen on 2 May on a non-electrified stretch of line at Kew Bridge, with the 'O' indicating that it is an inter-regional working whose destination is the SR. Seen from the cab of the 10.06 EMU from Waterloo, No. 118 has a heavy load behind it, judging by the heaps of coal visible above the sides of the wagons. Note the somewhat lacklustre architecture in this part of south London.

# 1973
## No 1 Records

**January**
Long haired lover from Liverpool          *Little Jimmy Osmond*
Blockbuster                                              *Sweet*

**March**
Cum on feel the noize                                    *Slade*
The twelfth of never                          *Donny Osmond*

**April**
Get down                                      *Gilbert O'Sullivan*
Tie a yellow ribbon round the old oak tree
                                              *Dawn/Tony Orlando*

**May**
See my baby jive                                       *Wizzard*

**June**
Can the can                                         *Suzi Quatro*
Rubber bullets                                            *10 cc*
Skweeze me, pleeze me                                    *Slade*

**July**
Welcome home                                   *Peters and Lee*
I'm the leader of the gang (I am)              *Gary Glitter*

**August**
Young love                                     *Donny Osmond*

**September**
Angel fingers                                         *Wizzard*
Eye level                               *Simon Park Orchestra*

**October**
Daydreamer                                    *David Cassidy*

**November**
I love you love me love                         *Gary Glitter*

**December**
Merry Xmas everybody                                    *Slade*

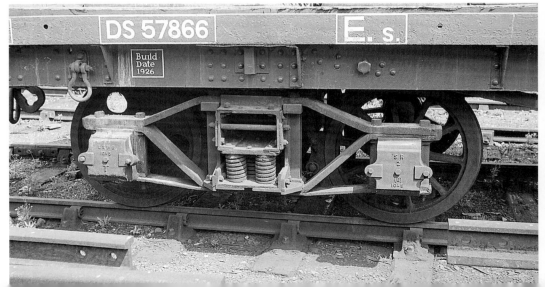

# 1973
## Finer details for railway modellers

*Opposite* **WATERLOO** Seen at Waterloo North Sidings on 29 June, 46-year old engineering wagon No. DS57866 – proudly stamped with its year of manufacture! – is the proud possessor of three distinct types of wheels! Careful inspection will show that the two left-hand wheels in these views are different to the right-hand ones (which are common to both views)! The axle box covers also show different 'owners' – L&SWR and the later SR.

*Right* **WATERLOO** A detail from a view at Waterloo North Sidings on 29 June, portrays a rather ancient-looking water column – presumably not in constant use as only diesels and electrics now enter the station area! – and a very 'ad hoc' trolley, one of a pair bearing lengths of wood and gas cylinders. By its appearance, the trolley could easily have come from the previous century!

*Below* **SANDHURST** Lineside and on-track details for the modeller. On 3 June, Ganger George Simpson is 'on guard' at Sandhurst, during a possession of the line for engineering work. Note the two styles of concrete workmen's huts, the train stopped in Sandhurst station in the distance and the red flags indicating 'Thou shalt not pass'! How different the scene to that which would pertain thirty years later!

*Below* **WINDERMERE** As already seen on.p12, the Windermere station, at the other end of the branch from Oxenholme is now but a very pale shadow of its former self. Some evidence of that former glory is seen in this view at 12.10 on 23 July, looking eastwards away from the buffer stops. Built in the mid-19th century, it was a grand affair, anticipating volumes of passenger traffic and at a time when railways were not ashamed of proclaiming their presence! By the time of our view however, only the nearest track is in constant use and the far side of the station is falling into disrepair. This near platform and its track is all that is now left in 2006, with no overhead cover!

*Above* **OXENHOLME** 'Change here for the Lakes'. In bright sunny conditions of late afternoon on 23 July, English Electric Type 4 (later BR Class 50) No. 433 slows for the Oxenholme stop as the 16.00 from Carlisle. Introduced by BR in 1968 for front line duties on the WCML, the spread of electrification out of Euston – see the overhead wires here and 87002 on pp. 21-24 – saw them replaced within just a few short years and moved to the WR by the end of the 1970s. 433 was named *Glorious* at Plymouth (Laira) depot on 26 June 1978 and although withdrawn on 25 March 1994 as one of the last of the class, preservation beckoned.

## 1973
### North to the Lakeside & Haverthwaite

*Left And below* **WINDERMERE** Moving to the southern end of Lake Windermere on 23 July, we see ex-LMS 'Stanier 4' 2-6-4T No. 2073 leaving Lakeside station on the private Lakeside & Haverthwaite Railway, while a 'Sealink Windermere' vessel *Swan* slows for docking at Lakeside Pier, close by the railway.

LAKE SIDE

SWAN

*Below* **HAVERTHWAITE** Engine movements are always a fascination – and not just for young boys! On 23 July, 2073 runs round its train, accelerating on the loop line as its passes under the footbridge. Note the 'LHR' on the rear of the coach, denoting ownership of the Lakeside & Haverthwaite Railway. Beyond the platform, there seems to be plenty of space for picnicking.

*Left* **HAVERTHWAITE** Captured by mother, father and daughter take a brief moment to examine 2073's motion before the train's departure on 23 July. Daughter's face seems to show some doubts, however, as to the wisdom of the enterprise!

*Below* **HAVERTHWAITE** The same day and ex-BR and industrial locomotives await their turn for attention at the side of Haverthwaite goods shed, including 'Black 5' No. 44806, a sometime resident of the Llangollen Railway.

**HAVERTHWAITE** The train on p.43 has arrived at Haverthwaite, at the other end of the line and 2073 has run round its stock and is ready for the next trip, the 1435 to Lakeside station. Note the very pleasant surroundings at this terminus, which have been further enhanced since this view.

# Trains and boats... but no planes!

*Upper* **HAVERTHWAITE** Once more 2073 starts away from Haverthwaite, this time with the 14.35 to Lakeside on 23 July. 'Sister' loco No. 2085 stands by the engine shed in the distance.

*Lower* **WINDERMERE** Another 'Sealink Windemere' vessel, Teal, smoothly glides towards Lakeside Pier, to meet the incoming train travellers.

# Index

## Acknowledgements

As with projects of any size and/or complexity, there are many people 'behind the scenes' who give of their time, expertise, advice, etc. willingly but often receive little in the way of thanks in return. The same is true with this new series, with the exception that the team putting the launch titles together has been smaller than is the norm.

There have been others 'in the wings', but the core personalities who deserve especial mention – apart from the two authors, whose patience, tolerance and friendship have somehow survived long hours, tight deadlines and frustration with some lack of information from the original photographs (!) – are Brian Morrison, for his constant and ever-ready willingness to offer assistance, advice and research facilities and for proof reading so quickly; and Sharon Rich, for her common sense approach and comments. This is her first excursion into the world of publishing and not only has it been eye-opener for her, but she has added a vital ingredient of not being an existing railway enthusiast! She has also coped remarkably well with those same tight deadlines, on top of managing her family and domestic duties!

Paul Shannon and John Vaughan deserve mention for specialist information on specific pictures.

Peter Rowlands is also thanked for his early enthusiasm, encouragement and for helping to drum up outside support; and Connie Ruffell for permission to use one or two specific photographs. Frances Townsend for sustaining her husband through the process! Without these individuals, the project would not have achieved what it already has.